*Neurodi**VERSE***

NeurodiVERSE

An anthology of poetry by neurodivergent writers

Eds. Janine Booth, Kate Fox,
Rob Steventon & Paul Neads

Flapjack Press

flapjackpress.co.uk

Exploring the synergy between performance and the page

Published in 2022 by Flapjack Press
Salford, Gtr Manchester
⊕ flapjackpress.co.uk f Flapjack Press
🐦 FlapjackPress ▶ Flapjack Press

⊕ janinebooth.com
⊕ katefoxwriter.wordpress.com
f robsteventonpoet

ISBN 978-1-8384703-1-9

Cover photo by McDobbie Hu on Unsplash
⊕ unsplash.com/@hjx518756

Printed by Imprint Digital
Exeter, Devon
⊕ digital.imprint.co.uk

MANCHESTER
A UNESCO City
of Literature

Contents

Introduction

Welcome, one and all, to *NeurodiVERSE*, an anthology of poetry featuring neurodivergent writers.

'Neurodiversity' is a term devised in 1998 by sociologist Judy Singer, acknowledging that humanity is neurologically diverse: that different people have different brain 'wiring' or structure. Acceptance of neurodiversity means embracing that there is not one 'normal' or 'correct' type of brain; that neurological difference occurs naturally and is an asset to our species.

Whilst we might call people with the most common form of brain 'neurotypical', those with a minority neurotype are 'neurodivergent'. This includes autistic, dyspraxic, dyscalculic and dyslexic people, and people with 'conditions' such as attention deficit hyperactivity disorder and Tourette syndrome – but there is no definitive list of conditions that 'count' as neurodivergent!

Sadly, our society persists in seeing neurodivergent people as faulty, as people to be written about and pitied rather than as people who write and speak for themselves. Society disables us even if our brains do not.

With contributions from over fifty poets, this is poetry *about* the neurodivergent experience specifically *by* neurodivergent writers. These poems showcase how each has used poetry to express themselves, explore their identities, ideas and feelings, and articulate their demands for rights and equality. This enables direct personal insight which can educate and move readers in ways that other media frequently fails to.

NeurodiVERSE aims to provide a powerful and diverse representation, with positive, authentic and progressive portrayals of life, countering ill-informed, unrepresented, misrepresented, pathologising and even pitying images elsewhere. The poems herein have been selected on the basis of quality, whilst ensuring that contributors include writers of various ages, genders, ethnicities and experiences. With accessibility a key tenet, this work is open to all who wish to learn about neurodiversity – and to all lovers of poetry.

The Editors
January 2022

Neurodi**VERSE**

GROWING UP

Noticing that you are different from other kids can be fascinating or bewildering. Your difference can be a delight or a pretext for bullying. Or both.

The structure of school requires a typical attention span, typical ways of communicating and learning, typical sensory sensitivities. If yours are atypical, you have 'special needs', and the funding to meet these is disappearing fast. It is little wonder that neurodivergent kids are far more likely to be excluded from school or to leave with low, or no, qualifications.

Neurodivergent children grow into neurodivergent adults, often to find very little recognition or support.

Natalie Jayne Clark is a neurodivergent writer, editor and teacher diagnosed with ADHD. They jointly lead a weekly reading session for Open Book and coordinated SYP Scotland's book club and shadow awards panel. Natalie's poetry has been displayed as part of Queer Dot's Synchronicity exhibition in three different cities across the UK and they are a member of The Scribbler's Union spoken word writing collective – co-editing their first anthology which reached № 7 on Amazon's poetry charts!

Laura Taylor has been writing and performing poetry since 2010. She is dyscalculic, with no formal diagnosis and struggles with all things number-related. She also suffered with an all-consuming form of OCD as a child, almost certainly as a result of maternal physical and mental abuse, and bullying outside of the home. Her third collection with Flapjack Press, *Speaking in Tongues*, was published in 2021.

Barry Fentiman Hall is a Medway-based poet whose books include *The Unbearable Sheerness Of Being* (Wordsmithery, 2016), *England, My Dandelion Heart* (Wordsmithery, 2018), and *Sketches* (Wordsmithery, 2020). He was born with spastic diplegia, although old notes just say cerebral palsy. His son and nephew are both on the autistic spectrum and he once asked his wife if she thought that he might be, to which she replied, "Oh yes dear, I very much think that you are...".

Lucy A. Snyder has inattentive type ADHD and lives in Columbus, Ohio. Over fifty of her poems have appeared in publications such as *Asimov's Science Fiction Magazine*, *Weirdbook*, *Vastarien* and *Nightmare Magazine*, and her latest collection is titled *Exposed Nerves*.

Sarah L. Dixon was born in Stockport and is based in a Huddersfield valley. She has autistic traits, overshares and makes too much eye contact to prevent her from getting easily distracted, and is overwhelmed by crowds, scents and other kinds of input. Her collections include *The Sky is Cracked* (2017), *Adding Wax Patterns to Wednesday* (2018) and *Aardvark Wisdom* (2021).

Thick Richard has performed on BBC Radio 4 and presented BBC Radio 6 Music's *Beat of the Day*. In 2017 he was part of a delegation with Dyslexia Institute UK which travelled to the European Parliament to propose a Dyslexia Charter. His second collection with Flapjack Press, *Read 'em and Weep*, was published in 2020 and he is currently writing a book about being a dyslexic writer and performer.

she's bright but she talks too much

a room of thirty
malleable minds and stretching flesh
two pupils stand out

he can't sit still – neither can i
he folds paper aeroplanes and makes them fly
my leg jogs and my doodles march
over the margins, across my hands and up my wrists

he finds it hard to be quiet – so do i
he makes animal noises and plane noises and fart noises
it *hurts* me to let someone else answer a question

he never finishes his work – i struggle too
despite our love of learning:
'sharp but needs to put in more effort'
is how we're described
ideas rush too much or our brains stall and stutter
no letter written looks much like another

we *both* receive recurring detentions for never doing homework
we *both* lose or crumple or forget our notes
we *both* have the occasional meltdown at the hint of negative
    feedback

we were in the same classes from the age of four to sixteen
guess who was diagnosed at eight
and who was diagnosed at nearly thirty?
you're right, the latter was me – the she

you see *he* fit the classic criteria of ADHD

i mean, look – i did too
but although our symptoms were often the same
his manifested in ways that affected others more
whilst mine often turned inwards or were hidden at home
masking and coping and pedalling faster
drowning in junk and shame

society's perceptions and expectations of our genders
are vastly, vastly different
not to mention the gender data gap
the lack of knowledge about the condition affects
                    e v e r y b o d y

only through other ADHD women on the internet
their honesty, their research, their silly humour
their campaigning to dispel myths
did i discover
why why why
i am the way i am

so i am going to take this chaotic energy
and fight and shout and teach and try
to make things right for others needing answers too

1977

Miss Fitzsimmons wasn't known for her tact.
My thigh still stings
for my crimes against maths;
discipline applied
to long division.

If *x* equals why
can't I work it out?
I am *wasting time* and if I carry on like that
I'll be in trouble.
Am I *daft?*

Telling time is telling lies.
4 is 20, 1 is 5, 2 is 10?
My arm is up again.
She combusts.
I'm *not trying hard enough,*
dunce.

Don't ask so many questions.
Troublemakers sit

                                   at the front

of each class;
every day, every week, every month, every year.
Have a think about that.

I'm not allowed to set the clock.
He says we're up at dawn
or on a verbal warning
if I do it. It's funny but
it's not haha.

Secret documents. Grown-up, office-based
help with 'Percentages', 'Petty Cash',
'How to do VAT in reverse'.
I manage panic
and sweat-soaked shame
at work.

Figures set fire to my *ignorant* face.
I bathe in words, balm
for my blistering brain.
I could read before the age of 3
but Miss still sits in my scrambling burn
and my adult thigh trembles
at the memory.

Barry Fentiman Hall

Earthbound Crow

I had forgotten somehow
        that I once had wings
The aches I get
        across my chest
            are muscle memories
      of a painful loss
My feet are planted
        firmer on the ground
      each passing year
An earthbound crow
        hopping three-toed
           to officiate
      on all that matters
    beneath the sky
We shed our feathers
        with our childhood
when we do not
      know their purpose
And only when
      our wings are gone
do we remember
        we can fly

The Wrong Daughter

Those two redheaded cousins down
in the holler maybe shared a daddy
or maybe nothing but the same bad taste
in dirty boots and boys with boosted cars.

Strangers argue but can't tell 'em apart.
Sometimes their own mamas mistake
Patsy for Addie at a squinting distance,
calling the wrong daughter to dinner.

But she ain't hungry; her mind is racing
burning neural blacktop day and night
nightmares spilling like sludgy motor oil
across the leather of her cracking soul.

The drive-in behind her eyes replays
the same grindhouse flick over and over.
Did relentless twitches put her in danger
or did hairy escapes give her the shakes?

Chicken and eggs are a scorchy mess
in her stepdaddy's red-hot iron skillet
and the slender man growls *Goddammit
I'll give you something to cry about.*

Magical Thinking

If this Loveheart lasts
until I am home
Indie Fringe will
smile at me in Maths

If I take exactly
383 steps from the school-gate
to my classroom door
Ecky will give me a Christmas card
and it will have a single 'x'

If I read until p18 of the *MEN*
while doing my paper round
Grey-coat-with-red-cuffs
will be washing his Mum's car

If I see my watch tick
over to the hour
each hour for a week
Baker will kiss me

If I kiss every Take That poster
(there are 108)
at a different time each night
for a year
Mark will want to marry me

If I cut through behind the tennis courts
3 times each way
even though it scares me
Brad-from-*Neighbours*
will be reading

on a deckchair
top off
eyes closed...

Thick Richard

EnglPHDish

I spent 16 years of my life
Learning how to read and <u>right</u>   } HOMOPHONE
But I learned how to read all wrong
And it soon became apparent
From studying the "3 R's"
Reading, R<u>w</u>iting, and R<u>RR</u>ithmatic   SP.
That someone somewhere was taking the piss with the
<u>englPHDish</u> language
For example...

Y
A
C   =   YOT   ✗
H   YOU AUGHT!
T

As in: "when your <u>sighning</u> on YACHT to be able to spell your
own fucking name properly"
So like some linguistic dickhead wizard
Casting spelling errors   MALAPHOR
<u>Srawled</u> like a sundried worm   SIMILÉ
<u>Corected</u> in <u>read</u> pen   PARANOMASIA
With a footnote that says ✳
D- and a sad face   A GREY DAY
It was a grade A when the exam results came   PUN!
But despite what the <u>teaches</u> told me
I am <u>self taught</u> in the art of word play
I take my nonsense very seriously   OXYMORON
And I now <u>actualy</u> have a PHD in <u>english</u>

This shit doesn't make sense! Are you doing your
homework drunk? It looks like you wrote it
with your fucking foot!   D— ☹
   JUST BECAUSE YOU SPELL THE WORD 'ENGLISH'
WITH A P, H + D DOES <u>NOT</u> MEAN YOU HAVE
ACHIEVED A PHD <u>IN THE SUBJECT OF</u> ENGLISH!!!

Every paragrahs a word search sliding off the padge
The letters grow little legs and try too run away _ALLITERATION_
Mocking me and my badly wired brain
As my toung tryes to chase them twisting like a snake
_?_

Was WH spooner simply playing it dumb
Id much sooner just be saying it wrong
Coz when you get muddled up with your dobble dutch
Youll find that mutch of your troubles start doubbleing up
The bus time table reads like an algerbra test
Bad granma to me is rosemary west _GRAMMAR!! X_
NOT QUITE A DOUBLE SPOONERISM, BUT NICE TRY
(when I started writing this poem I decided to cram as much
word play as I could into it, spoonerisims, redundacys,
malaphors, oxymorons, blah blah blah, and I soon regreted
it because coming up with this shit by accident is all good
and well but when you acctualy try to turn that tap on the
creative juces run dry pretty fucking quick ! but I was
detrmend to write a palindrome. For those of you who dont
know a palindrome is a word or phrase that reads the same
forwards as it dose backwards. Symmetrical spelling, For
example: ✓
"madam I'm Adam" ✓
"if I had a hifi"
"tit" (and coincidenty "boob" witch is unusual when you _?_
consider how rarely they are symmetrical in real life, yet it
seams to work on paper, and that's nice !)
But im happy to say after 3 moths in dyslexia hell I managed
to write a 10 word palindrome !!!!!!!! and here it is...)

"the palindrome originates from the small welsh town of X
Fonwothslewllamsehtmorfsetanigiroemordnilapeht"

My aunty Joan insisted on pronouncing the word scone as "scone"
So now I call her aunty John

— 23 —

To be <u>honst</u> I find most dyslexics do my fucking head in, <u>self important</u> <u>sonbs</u> who think they've been touched by the hand of some creative god just because they "<u>cant</u> read good". The type of big heads who spout nonsense like "oh, well, <u>einstine</u> was a dyslexic don't you know!" And that's just the type of <u>lodgic</u> <u>einstien</u> strived for isn't it "<u>einstine</u> was a dyslexic therefore: all dyslexics are German"

[handwritten: TWO REDUNANCIES IN ONE LINE!? X]

Page after <u>padge</u> of inane inanity

Not one word spelt the way <u>its</u> <u>ment</u> to be

All <u>fonetikalee</u>

It looks correct to me *[handwritten: X]*

I can only read it if its writ dick-lick-sickly *[handwritten: X]*

(<u>jeez</u>, <u>im</u> so dyslexic if you look up the word <u>dyslexica</u> in the dictionary <u>its</u> got a picture of me.) *

<u>Punkture</u> in the punch line the joke falls flat *[handwritten: SATIRICL! X]*

<u>Incohearent</u> <u>hyrogliphic</u> <u>clap trap</u>

cryptic <u>cross words</u> making me mad

<u>Im</u> a dyslexic and you're a twit x

[handwritten: ?! X]

* Next to the word bicycle.

HOME & FAMILY

Most people do not learn about neurodivergence until it makes itself known among their friends or family. Parents, carers and significant others may struggle with little support or understanding and precious few resources and services.

There is a heritable component to neurotypes, and so neurodivergent people may well have similarly neurodivergent relatives. They may find understanding and comradeship at home – or they may find rejection or efforts to 'normalise' them.

Social institutions often talk over us to our families, seeking their views not ours. We want our families and friends to be heard, but we want to be heard as well.

Henry Normal is founder of the Manchester Poetry (now Literature) Festival and co-founder of the Nottingham Poetry Festival. He has written extensively for TV, including co-writing *The Mrs Merton Show*, *The Royle Family* and the *Paul and Pauline Calf Video Diaries*. In 1999 he founded Baby Cow Productions Ltd and Executive Produced all and script edited many of their shows, receiving a special Bafta for services to television in 2017. Highlights of his tenure as MD include *Alan Partridge*, *Nighty Night*, *The Mighty Boosh*, *Gavin and Stacey* and the Oscar-nominated *Philomena*. Since 2016, Henry has written and performed several BBC Radio 4 shows for his acclaimed and ongoing series *A Normal* ..., combining poetry, comedy and stories about his life and family.

Brendan Curtis is a neurodivergent chef, performer and drag artist. He co-facilitates *Queer Bodies Poetry* and *Eat Me* (a drag dinner cabaret), and writes about queer stuff, small beautiful things and the grotesque.

Philippa Blakey has the inattentive version of adult ADHD. She is a single parent to a potentially ADHD 12-year-old and is currently working in schools as a one-to-one mentor for struggling children, many of whom have neurodivergent diagnosis or undiagnosed tendencies.

Karl Knights is an autistic writer with cerebral palsy. He was a winner of the 2021 New Poets Prize and his poetry and prose has appeared in *Poetry London*, *The Guardian* and *The Dark Horse*. His debut pamphlet, *Kin*, is forthcoming from the Poetry Business.

Olivia Tuck's poetry has appeared in print and online journals including *The Interpreter's House*, *Lighthouse Journal* and *Ink Sweat & Tears*, as well as *Tears in the Fence*, where she is an editorial intern. Her pamphlet, *Things Only Borderlines Know*, focuses on her experiences of living with mental illness and autism and is published by Black Rabbit Press. Her poem

'Developmental History' considers part of the assessment process for autism diagnosis, whereby a developmental history is often taken from adult family members who knew the patient as they grew up.

Spencer Mason is a writer and musician diagnosed with schizoaffective disorder and complex PTSD, as well as being a recovering addict. He is undertaking a Creative Writing MA at Manchester Metropolitan University whilst living in Glasgow.

Summer on Pluto

In a room with no windows
I am given a leaflet

The word **incurable**
is printed in bold on the first page

This is the only time I will spend in this room
This is the only time I will speak to this person

Autism is a spectrum
there are degrees

Your son is mildly severe
What does that mean?

It means he will always live at home
it means he will never have a job

never have a girlfriend
never be capable of taking care of himself

You will never have a conversation with him
ever

It means you will worry about him every day
you will worry if he's happy

you will worry if he's lonely
you will worry what will happen to him when you die

Mildly severe
benignly savage

kindly cruel
none of this appeared on the leaflet

Brendan Curtis

the pond

my father was always working
like joseph the carpenter
sometimes emerge sweating from the workshop
to feed

run away from us
in supermarkets
on long foreign holidays
massage parlour
as i hollowed out the innards of baguettes

the raised bed vegetable patch
the conservatory
the japanese waterfall garden
with metamorphic rocks
imported at a steal
from somewhere
far away
it was my job
to water the green house:
leopard spotted spiders
webbing at every join or intersection
still flinch at
the stems of tomatoes
their green upside-down bodies
my mother's favourite smell

i would sit
by the pond talking
to the newts in popped bubbles from my lips
lifted the stagnant liquid out

in a life-full bucket to study
when i tripped on the door jamb
spilled the whole thing
rage of my parents
was worse than the sulphurous
black gunk stain
all over the new grey carpet

when we had to move
due to
financial misconduct
(a false company was created
in my name)
listening to
a newer, richer family
walking around the house
they talked loudly about everything
that would be different:
so-and-so
did not want a pond

i remember
the truck arriving:
large corrugated hose
wound through the back door
like an anaconda
father:
disappeared
to mourn

the machine
took an hour
to suck out
every drop:

giant slurping
the last dregs
of a milkshake
with a straw
this was
the first time
i understood
apocalypse:

squirming
black sludge
seeming to gasp
for breath
as it dried into
oil-like scum

Philippa Blakey

Tick Here for Single Parent Household

There are rarely single purpose journeys.
Some are no purpose;
bewildered meanderings,
poorly regulated attempts to
flush out the cortisol,
rock the pain
back and forth.
Pacing a disarming dining room
of half-finished situations,
of breaks and breakthroughs,
shame and order,
delight and disarray.
The kitchen calls
without much clarity,
whilst the washing basket
makes a distant case.
I meet an adult here sometimes
who could write you
3000 words of sparkling
praxis in 72 hours,
who persuades whole
groups of appliances
to hum compliant,
who lights candles
and waters plants.
I saw her hoovering beams once
and I thought;
"My god. You are incredible."
Go on, finish that book/meal/thought/conversation/
career plan/relationship/therapy.
You deserve it.

Karl Knights

Great Nanny

Dad carries me up the stairs to her flat.
As soon as he's gone she hands me a pair
of headphones so I can ignore her chirping budgie.
She doesn't insist on looking her in the eye, or giving
her a hug. She knows I'm always listening. To her,
I'm Karl Knights, no inside voice and perfect
crooked bones. She tells me about Margaret
from Iceland again. We play Snap but I go slow
to let her win. She never slammed her hand down
and yelled 'Snap!', it was always a small laugh
and two wrinkled knuckles would tap the cards.
When it's time to leave she gives me a pound.
I go down the stairs on Dad's shoulders,
holding her coin between my fingers.

Olivia Tuck

Developmental History

Daddy wore new trousers; Mummy left her posh-girl pupils
to go to you, Doctor. I've seen the conversation's remains –
its exoskeleton looks like crushed ice.
Was there a game of twenty questions? Fifty?

More? I understand you asked them about my past
obsessions with spiralling car wash brushes;
with lighthouses on headlands. But I was exiled,
held at school so I wouldn't spill on your carpet.

I hope you could all feel the poltergeist
of me, simmering. I want you to have blinked
and listened to the clock's bradycardia; squinted
into violent sun that howled through the panel in the door,

down chalk tracks, to a History classroom,
where my skirt climbed laddered nylon against fat thigh,
tears scalding the pus-filled stars across my cheeks,
bloody lipstick pooling on my chin.

My Unfortunate Daughter

Come my dearest sweet,
come willing with a smoke,
come sit yourself by the fire here
and help yourself tae toke.
Can you see these flames, my dear,
as they dance in tribute to you,
or do you perceive the anger, dear,
from when they took all lust had left to lose?

I mind as you got older, girl,
learned all of your own accord,
but you always kept Dundee's rebel heart:
you never did what you were told.
You always slept so sound and sweet,
forever dreaming, true and bold –
but I know the nights have gotten darker
as you have gotten old.

They considered it genetics, dear;
I gave thee all I had to give,
and all those that have plagued me
are now in your soul to live.
I know you cry at night, my brave,
I know the terrors and the fright.
I know those voices that convene, connive,
convince you of what's 'right'.

They have been around a while, my dear,
I have seen this all before.
I know these things you feel and fear,
that your heart has become torn

between moral questions of deserving love,
your callousness doubting you'll be enough
to find a suitor, humble and of honest heart,
who hears your songs like pure white doves.

I ken such things can always be
as you beg and barter with your fear
to fade, to gratify your plea;
you must not be captive, my dear,
lest you ever doubt yourself –
let your dreams be courage to reap.
And I will stay here beside the fire, my dear,
I will stand guard as you sleep.

WORK

Just 21.7% of working-age autistic adults are in paid work, the lowest rate of all disability categories (Source: Office for National Statistics). People with ADHD are twice as likely to have been dismissed from a job than people without (Source: AttentionUK).

Work is organised to maximise profit, usually structured in strict and hierarchical ways with little control by workers, presenting difficulties to those who think differently.

Many trade unions are taking up the issue of neurodiversity in the workplace, demanding more accessible and inclusive workplaces and supporting individual workers.

To paraphrase Karl Marx, neurodivergent workers have thus far had to navigate, suffer or avoid the workplace – the point, however, is to change it.

Janine Booth is an autistic speaker, tutor, poet and socialist activist. Her many published works include *Autism Equality in the Workplace* (Jessica Kingsley Publishers, 2016), *Minnie Lansbury: suffragette, socialist, rebel councillor* (Five Leaves, 2018), *The Big J vs The Big C* (Flapjack Press, 2019) and *Fighting Tories: The Force Awakens* (Roundhead, 2020). Janine also curated the anthology *CoronaVerses: Poems from the Pandemic*.

Robert Garnham is a performance poet, recently diagnosed as dyslexic. He has taken several shows to fringes and festivals, and in 2017 was mentioned as having one of the funniest jokes of the Edinburgh Fringe. Robert also writes short stories, humour essays and a regular newspaper column in the South West.

Andy N was registered with dyspraxia at the age of 29 and is the author of six poetry collections, the most recent being *Haiku of Life*. He co-runs the spoken word open mic night Speak Easy, has a regular column on the *Sunday Tribune*, and does a variety of podcasts.

Steven Waling took an online autism test in which he came out as 'borderline' autistic, but without an actual diagnosis would not lay claim to the label. Having worked with neurodivergent people, he feels many lives are made worse by trying to conform to 'normality'. His latest collection, *Lockdown Latitudes*, was recently published by Leafe Press.

Keeks Mc lives and works in Glasgow with her young family, and recently discovered through her job in public service that she likely has ADHD. Although still awaiting a formal diagnosis, at 40, this has allowed her to rationalise and appreciate her approach to life. Her poems address neurodiversity and reflect her personal and family's experiences of functioning in a neurotypical world. Her vernacular poem 'Coungerin the Gliff' is accompanied by a guiding translation.

Rob Steventon is a dyslexic and dyspraxic stand-up poet, champion of Manchester's Word War and York's Say Owt poetry slams, and founder of Punk in Drublic Poetry – the Saboteur Award-winning night with all door fees donated to Mustard Tree Homelessness charity. His debut collection, *How I Made My Millions*, was published by Flapjack Press in 2021.

Janine Booth

We Had to Let Them Go

He worked alone, not a team player
Not a keeper or a stayer
Didn't fit in, not really our sort
Talked about boring stuff not sport
We had to let him go

She didn't smile, service with a frown
Missed the big picture, always drilling down
Flapped her hands, rocked and hummed
Chewed her pen and sucked her thumb
We had to let her go

Profit margins were getting low
We didn't want to let him go
But some things we just can't afford
We can't keep funding his support
So we had to let him go

Wasn't friendly – never spoke
Lost her temper – can't take a joke
Had some really weird obsession
Didn't give a good impression
We had to let her go

She wouldn't put in the extra hours
No party tricks or superpowers
Too quiet – too loud – too fast – too slow
Everyone said she had to go

Great at the actual job, to be fair
Well, yeah
But we had to let them go

On a poet discovering he's dyslexic
just before his 47th birthday

It's not that the words danced around,
It's just that there were too many of them,
Some sentences so convoluted
My head would shut down
Like a fizz of static on an old TV,
I'd overheat,
Sweat pouring from my brow.

I'm a poet, right?
Words are meant to be my playthings.
But it just felt more that they were
Playing with me,
Toying with me,
Hiding the truth behind the very words
Which the more competent people around me were using
To convey that very truth.
Doesn't a bad worker
Always blame his tools?

In management meetings,
Words,
Too many of them,
Too many concepts,
Too much abstraction
Piled and peppered in paragraphs on the page,
They'd bland themselves into the blandground
And I'd try to pick them out,
Catch them, these
Multisyllabic monsters plucked
Between thumb and forefinger,

And I'd scream,
"I know what you mean individually!
But together,
It's all nonsense!
For goodness sake, just behave!"

And I'd leave the meeting,
The lesson, the symposium, the convention,
The workshop, the lecture, the presentation
Hot and sweaty and thinking
Everyone around me were superheroes
Because they understood everything at the very first attempt.
"And now we come onto
Socio-economic considerations in means tested arts funding
Community-based stakeholder applications."
And I'd
Have absolutely no idea,
And I'd ask someone
And they knew every nuance
So I'd pretend that I did too.

Perhaps I always knew something were amiss.
I could never take directions, or phone calls,
Or even simple instructions without
Writing it down and re-reading it five, six, seven times.
Now just slow down, slow down,
Let me write this, let me make some notes,
What do you mean you're not going over it a second time?
Those bloody words again!
You're meant to be my friends!

Sure, I can write like no-one's business
And tap dance on the precipice of literary expression.
But open my mouth
And I'm as erudite as a stunned slug.

You see that line that I just wrote there?
I could never have uttered that in real life.
It takes me the best part of the morning
To come up with something so spontaneous.

This whole time,
I thought that words were my friends.
But close my eyes and they dance.
It turns out
They were always there.
They were just cheating on me.

Between Then and Now
(A life before and after the discovery of dyspraxia)

They never said I was stupid in my exams at secondary
but I knew from the results I got back with the letter U
staring at me in the face or marks that weren't much better
they would have dismissed me as a waste of space.

They never said at work when at a warehouse or grocers
after leaving school on a Youth Training Scheme
even when I struggled to read where to file everything
and sent me back just saying I wasn't right.

Post room operative, kitchen porter
drifted through my teens and twenties
buried in confusion like tangled curtains over words
fighting through evening classes to re-educate myself.

Churning into the first year at university
grasping through the wastelands of sleep
spending twice as long as everybody else with essays
blackmailing myself to carry on with guilt

Marooned with dyspraxia my lecturer said I was
the word turning over in my tongue in the rain
pulling the outline of my life out into the open
instead of simply kicking the ladder away again,

changing the tune of the song
halfway through unmapping the mysteries
in the fog of my thoughts
with a slow in-take of breath of relief

and stopping me driving back
through the rain again alone.

Disrupt Me

Alone at the table   don't come and disrupt me

  Happy adding his figures   should be learning
  employment skills   sometimes I let him subtract
  he'd do it all day if allowed

My head's in a book   pen to paper don't interrupt

  Can't understand why he needs to map
  the route from his home to here   knows
  where he lives   catches the bus   (who'd
  want to visit

                    Anyway

            a train of thought arrives
at the station with its crowd of Saturday images
and I try to arrange them   all jumbled up
pieces of different jigsaws

  and he can't see why he needs to move
  that pile of boxes here   to there

            Meanwhile
the ongoing battle between the right and left
hemispheres of the brain
                    keeps me awake nights

  When asked to do something he can't
  see a reason   he cries
                    no-one explains
  the mystery of normal

And all the time I'm talking to you
I'm working on ways to appear
like I know what I'm doing

      so they send him on work placement
      to chalk another failure on his board

and I do the online test
                      come up borderline

      and we really must learn the skills
      to fit in the workplace

          and I want to do better
but it might be the reason   I fail at relationships

             it's really no excuse
so when you see me again   walk up to the table

disrupt me

Keeks Mc

Coungerin the Gliff

Sittin doon tae stert the darg
baith interestit an keen
tae dae a bang up joab
Ah manage tae scribe
mibbe twa lines
whan Ah suddenly stert wunnerin
whit the current temperatur in Chile is
an hou a rabbit keechs
in tottie wee roon baws
Shove it oot ma heid an cairy oan
Anither line doon
Ma mynd screams tae chack ma phone
Gae oan, gae oan
Althou it's no mad a peep an
Ah ainly chackt it nae mair
than three meenits aback
Whit's that? Ah'm hungry?
Sakes, Ah jist ate ma brakfast
Ramsh shite onyway
than laith masel
but nanetheless decree the seal
is broke fur the day sae onythin gaes
in a clood o contermacious temerity
Noo Ah'm wunnerin hou much a wadset
oan a hoose Ah kid neer afford wid be
Chack phone
Muse at rearrangin the hoose
Chack sel
In the name o fuck wumman
scribe that email
Yeve ainly twa lines tae gae

An sae it repeats a day
Tryin tae lui tae the daily cas
Gie tent tae ma wean an ma man
Hell kens Ah'm mair than interestit
but thare's sae much
circlin roon in ma heid tae dae an think aboot
it's owerwhalmin
An if Ah'm bad wi chocolate
Ah'm wurst wi drink
Aye, Ah'll jist want the wan
But twa hoors an hauf a dozen lairge wans later
it seems a gey guid idee
tae gae tae a club in a faur awa city
or veesit an auld dear freen
That's hou Ah drink nae mair
A day, ivry day is the faircest battle
agin Masel, ma naitural wills
A the whiles, abody thinks yer fordersome
an a bit unfarrent
It's gey exowstin

Translation –
Beating the Impulses

Sitting down to start the day's work
both interested and keen
to do a brilliant job
I manage to write
maybe two lines
when I suddenly start wondering
what the current temperature in Chile is
and why a rabbit poos
in tiny wee round balls
Shove it out my head and carry on
Another line down
My mind screams to check my phone
Go on, go on
Although it's not made a sound
and I only checked it no more
than three minutes ago
What's that? I'm hungry?
Sakes, I just ate breakfast
Munch shite anyway
Then hate myself
But nonetheless decree the seal
Is broken for the day
So anything goes
In a cloud of obstinate temerity
Now I'm wondering how much a mortgage
on a house I could never afford would be
Check phone
Must at rearranging the house
Check self
In the name of fuck woman
write that email
You've only two lines to go

And so it repeats all day
Trying to listen to the daily calla
Giving attention to my child and husband
Hell knows I'm more than interested
But there's so much
circling round in my head to do and think about
it's overwhelming
And if I'm bad with chocolate
I'm worst with drink
Yes I'll just want the one
but two hours and half a dozen large ones later
It seems a really great idea
To go to a club in a far off city
or visit an old dear friend...
That's why I drink no more
All day, everyday is the fiercest battle
against myself, my natural impulses
All the while everyone thinks you're impetuous
and a little bit rude
It's really exhausting

Rob Steventon

Access to Work

To whom it may concern.

Please see attached to read and take into consideration
Our client's needs assessment from which we make
  recommendations.
Our client is in hope that they will meet full implementation.
Our client gave his consent for us to share this information.

Our client tells us that he holds a firm commitment to his work,
His responsibilities to those he serves he will not shirk.
Amidst the mist of tentativeness, he's tenacious but now irked
By insidious cynicism on him, management besmirched.

We're here to convey his support needs and provide some
  helpful pointers
To increase your awareness, which of course seems to be
  cloistered.
He reports he's asked for adjustments and just been left to
  loiter
Until the workload shit hits client's fan, at which point he's
  exploited.

Having asked for clearer instructions, feeling doomed to fail,
Puzzled why his manager 'replied all', chiding him in an email.
He's floated forth in leaky raft, equipped with a ripped-up sail
And told to learn to navigate whilst battling a gale.

Your poorly explained tasks, the worst possible cards, you're
  dealing
With his focus dwarfed by disorientated doomy feelings.
When sensitivity to aural stimuli leaves client reeling
You amplify your obnoxious office singing, while he's concealing

A determination outgunned, and frustrations escalating.
Feeling undermined, you've ignored the needs that he's been
stating.
When he confided when he reads, text appears to be oscillating,
You joked in front of the whole team that he must be
hallucinating.

When *patronise*, *dismiss* and *scrutinise* are your three favourite
tactics
In managing a worker who's trying to bear being dyspraxic,
Your attitude and approach have become at best problematic.
Please see our specific suggestions we hope you adopt in
practice.

— Your indiscreet haranguing over 5-minute lateness
should cease immediately. For our client, grasping time
can be like grasping the handlebars on a bicycle whilst
lathered in butter and our findings are that this has come
at a significantly higher cost to him than to you. The
working time deficit amounts to hours owed by employer
to employee on account of the dozens of hours of unpaid
overtime he has given. On this basis, **we suggest a pay-
out equivalent to two months' salary** to compensate
for said overtime, and for the indignity of being harangued
over such inconsequential matters in a public way.

— A screen overlay, adaptive software, instructions in flow-
chart format and greater consideration of the unnecessary
noise you make when singing in the office are reasonable
adjustments, not things that our client should be bullied
into feeling privileged for having granted, or things that he
should have insinuated will be paid for by deductions from
his salary. **We suggest you gain a greater
understanding of our client's condition and what
constitutes reasonable adjustments for this.**

— Other members of our client's team understanding instructions to a task more quickly than our client is not a sign of our client's inadequacies, it is a sign that you have not considered his needs. **We suggest you apologise in presence of the full team for the inadequacies in your own approach to management.**

— Your patronising insinuations that our client is either dim or lazy cease immediately, as aside from being completely superfluous to the remit of a manager, they are damaging, demeaning and discriminatory. **We suggest you wind your fucking neck in with these.**

Please do not hesitate to contact us for any further information relating to this.

Warmest regards,
The Access to Work Team

FITTING IN

We don't fit in. We are not 'normal'. But is there really such a thing as 'normal'? If everyone were the same, the world would be very boring. Neurodivergent people often find ourselves 'on the outside', through explicit prejudice or social exclusion.

We may behave in unusual ways; for example, 'stimming', carrying out self-stimulatory actions such as flapping or skipping that help us to regulate. We might not even fit the stereotype of a typical atypical person! Not every autistic person is a nerdy white boy, not every person with Tourette's shouts swear words.

Intolerance causes discrimination and distress in encounters with the justice system. Our difference becomes guilt. Our lack of eye contact arouses suspicion. The way we answer questions is misinterpreted to incriminate us.

Maddi Crease is an autistic poet from South East England. She writes about mental health and neurodivergency, and her work focuses on breaking barriers and questioning stereotypes, as well as aiming to make the unseen feel seen and the unheard heard.

Jill Abram is Director of Malika's Poetry Kitchen, a collective encouraging craft, community and development. She grew up in Manchester, travelled the world, and now lives in Brixton. Her publishing credits include *The Rialto*, *Magma*, *Poetry Scotland* and *Poetry Wales*, and she has performed at Ledbury Poetry Festival, StAnza Festival in Paris, and the USA. Jill produces and presents a variety of poetry events including the Stablemates series of poetry and conversation.

Kathryn O'Driscoll is a poet, writer and activist from Bath. She is the UK Slam Champion and a World Slam Finalist, and was part of the BAFTA-winning spoken word show *Life & Rhymes*. Her poetry openly addresses disabilities, mental health, living with a personality disorder, LGBTQIA+ issues and gender politics.

Graham Rodgers was diagnosed with Asperger's at the age of 20. His writing of his experiences was included in National Autistic Society's 'I Exist' campaign, the findings of which shaped the Autism Act of 2009. He subsequently founded the Swadlincote Asperger's Society, and is now a member of the Derbyshire Autism Partnership Board.

Margaret Corvid is a neurodivergent, socialist writer in Plymouth. Her first book of poems, *Singing in the Dark Times*, is published by Patrician Press.

Sarah Grant is a disabled researcher who was diagnosed as autistic in 2016 and is studying for a PhD on autism and chronic illness at King's College, London. She has been writing poetry, prose and music since age three, but seldom shares it with others.

Maddi Crease

Autistagirl

You say
My autism is my superpower.

I get it. The concept.
Autistic girl kinda sounds like 'autistagirl',
Right? Like, superhero name is the slogan for my existence,
Right? Like,
I'll be supergirl,
You'll be holder of pedestal,
Right?

Like, I'll be sweating out my best performance,
You'll be hoping I don't crash the whole dammed town,
Like I'll be hiding away
And you'll be exposing me.
Right?

Truth is,
I'm no hero,
No bearer of cape,
No powered one.
I am just a girl.

Just an autistic girl
Asking you
To see me.

But you call my autism:
Superpower.

You tell me I am more than human,
But all I hear is I am not person.
Not at all.

Jill Abram

Pretender

Natalia has a flat stomach and a cleavage.
She runs a mile without breaking a sweat.
Heads turn even when she's dressed in rags.

People recognise Natalia and remember
her name. When she speaks, they listen.
All her messages get prompt replies.

Natalia never waits to get served at the bar,
cars stop to let hers out. She gets voted
into office, sought out on Saturday nights.

Natalia's paintings hang in homes of people
she's never met; certificates hang in her own.
She has more letters after her name than in it.

Natalia is always first up and cheerful.
Her book is on the school curriculum.
Natalia can quote Keats.

Mutant

I am a mutant.
My skin does not sallow in the sun
and I do not blush jaundice through my cheeks.
I do not have extra fingers or toes –
although my spine;
it boasts an ironic vertebrae,
it is a long tally of the hearts I have broken
and when I straighten my spine the bones
pop out of place.
I am out of place.

I do not have a super power,
I lack exceptionality in all but my ordinariness.
There is a vengeful bacteria feasting –
on my shoulder places;
between the weight of the world,
the rock and the hard place,
a monster chews the fat and fetid flesh,
it laughs at me.
They laugh at me.

Deep in the equilibrium of my thoughts
hides a parasitic truth, grinding its teeth on mine;
it tugs at the tendons behind my eyeballs –
the puppeteer, it controls me.
It deceives and divides me
and floods my eyes and mind with doubt.
I am blinded by it and my cloudy eyes
see normality.
I seek normality.
I am a mutant.

Graham Rodgers
Confessions of a Stimmer

I am the painter,
Hands brushing – jabbing – scraping.

I am the conductor,
Arms reaching – pointing – waving.

I am the pianist,
Fingers poking – tapping – drumming.

I am the dancer,
Legs pacing – twisting – stomping.

I am the vocalist,
Lips cussing – whistling – scatting.

I am the imposter,
Mask covering – acting – faking.

Margaret Corvid

Autistic Women

So very few are kind to us, that we
gasp, like a person struggling for air
inside, all while pretending we don't care;
this happens all the time. We try to be
withholding to ourselves, to lie and mask
each gesture, each reaction, each reply
in normal clothes. We rarely think to ask
ourselves if this is fair. We wonder why
the older we become, the less we can
keep up with all the acting. It's because
our hearts, like brakes, begin to screech just when
the layers have worn off. Way back, it was
a thrill, to take the lie so very far.
But now, it seems we don't know who we are.

Sarah Grant

Falling Apart

sometimes, bits of me fall off
then i have to put that bit of me
in the freezer
wait till it's hardened a little
then stick it back on with superglue
this has happened
so many times now
that i'm starting to wonder if
i might be more
glue
than person
and what happens when there is nothing left
to fall off
but for now
i think i'm going to need a bigger freezer

MY BRAIN

Neurodivergent brains work in atypical ways. Not flawed or faulty, they are wired or structured differently from the majority. They may process at different speeds and focus in different ways, they may prefer words to numbers or vice versa.

This brings strengths as well as challenges. For example, evidence shows that dyslexic people have spatial reasoning abilities significantly better than average, perhaps explaining why the late Richard Rogers and so many other dyslexic people are successful architects. But we still name this neurotype after the commonly-known difficulty with written words; we don't call it 'enhanced spatial reasoning syndrome'!

Brain science is still in its early days. We hope that developing knowledge about the natural variation in human neurology brings more acceptance and appreciation of this difference.

Ann Penn lives in the East Midlands and was diagnosed in her forties as being autistic, which had led her to a greater understanding of her life. She is proud to be neurodivergent and to have found her community, and inspired to write poetry by Writing East Midlands' Beyond The Spectrum workshops which are run for and by autistic people.

Crake Eades is an autistic polymath who holds four degrees in different subjects, can make furniture and rewire a house, but often fails to hold down a job. She runs Gorilla Poetry, a monthly open mic in Sheffield.

Jeff Price is dyslexic and dyspraxic and he has passed this gift on to his daughters. He founded Poetry Vandals and ran Radikal Words CIC, working in schools, prisons and community centres, running workshops, writers' groups and performance poetry events. He now organises The Great Northern Slam at Northern Stage and regularly performs throughout the UK and South West of France. His collections include *Doors* [2006], *Toe in The Tarn* [2012] and *Infinite Threads* [2021] (a collaboration with photographer Chris Collister), and has released a CD/Book titled *Live at La Sirene*.

Vicky Morris is autistic with ADHD and dyslexia. Her poetry explores experiences of executive dysfunction and sensory processing issues. Her debut pamphlet, *If All This Never Happened*, was published by Southwords in 2021.

Lucy Power is a poet, artist and musician based in Manchester. She trained as a fine artist, but her multiple sclerosis began to limit her practice and so looked for other ways to make art. Now studying for a Masters in Creative Writing, her poems explore rural and urban situations peopled with diverse human and non-human characters.

Zoë Sîobhan Howarth-Lowe is a poet and mum from Dukinfield, Greater Manchester. She grew up assuming she was just the weird kid, never realising it could be neurodivergence until a teacher invited her to a meeting to discuss one of her children potentially being on the autistic spectrum.

Alain English is a Scottish actor and writer based in London. He trained at the International School of Screen Acting and has published two books of poems and one memoir. He is artist-in-residence at the Tea House Theatre, where he founded Paper Tiger Poetry, and speaks and performs regularly at autism events in London and across the UK.

John G. Hall is a Manchester poet, editor and workshop facilitator whose work considers the politics of PTSD and depression associated with serial bereavement and isolation.

Ann Penn

Thought Experiment

Nothing will change between today and tomorrow
apart from our knowledge.
For us, the experiment is still in progress,
but the result is already fixed.

The pendulum is held taut mid-swing
and my stomach is rigid as well,
tense for the rollercoaster swoop of gravity.
The carriage is preparing to set off,
and we will discover if we will soar or drop.

I am a fly trapped in amber, frozen in this moment of time,
existing in a state of suspended animation.
If I had a choice, I don't know which I'd pick –
staying in limbo, waiting for judgement,
or leaping into the unknown future.

I've always hated uncertainty,
so the answer should be easy.
Yet I've had ten years to practise living with this stage,
and I fear that new knowledge now
will merely bring more change and trauma.

But we have no say in this. The result is already fixed
and nothing we can do can change it.
The sand in the egg timer has nearly run through
and we must march onwards towards tomorrow
and open the box to discover the truth.

Crake Eades

I Have a Fancy Brain

When I look at the sky it sparkles.
Crushed diamonds moulded and shifting,
I thought everyone saw it this way.
Seeing patterns in the wallpaper,
Rivers flowing through texts,
Lines and objects seeming oddly flat.
But it stops life feeling flat.
I have a fancy brain that sparkles,
Reads odd meanings into texts;
It often feels like the world is shifting.
Whilst I try to fade into the wallpaper
I walk an odd meandering way.
Always lost, I try to find my way.
Wishing my mood was more flat,
Without needing soothing, gazing at wallpaper.
But then normality shines with sparkles,
With possibilities magically shifting,
And I enjoy living within the subtexts.
My lives are postmodern texts
Without one theme dictating the way.
Priorities change as focus seems shifting.
I'm unable to follow one route. Just flat.
Because I'm chasing fairies and sparkles
That hide in the cracks and paint the wallpaper.

I always see faces in the wallpaper
As if they are clues. Secret texts.
To a way to a life full of sparkles.
One day I feel I will find my way,
Away from where the landscape is flat,
To where the horizon is constantly shifting.

Because my mind keeps on shifting,
Ideas flowing from my head. Coating the wallpaper
With rivulets of thought which stand proud of the flat.
Written across the walls as hieroglyphic texts.
My mind has always wandered this way.
I have a fancy brain that sparkles.

Making a Spectacle of Yourself

As a child his fat spectacles would
frequently slip from his pustulated face
Picked last at school sports with a reputation
as the world's worst goalkeeper

Cockeyed pictures on pub's wall
distract him to the point of anger
He will make a mental note to bring
a spirit level to the next Friday night out

He would prefer a world where beauty
was literal and people were honest
Deviousness can catch his ankles
and send him crashing to the ground

He takes an eternity to be spontaneous
and can quickly prevaricate
He can feel awkward and unsure
in the company that he so often craves

Words dance on book pages and the order
of their letters often eludes him
But he loves them with a passion
it took him years to acknowledge

His world is a one-man play where he has
many parts, none of them suit him
Yet he is the sum of all of them
and an eager apprentice at each one in turn

Vicky Morris

German Train

I wish my mind was like this German train,
with its neat fold-up storage, deep luggage racks,
easy-reach wall hooks. Plenty of leg room.
Each seat with its own plug socket,
little boxes attached for all the rubbish.

And wide aisleways, no waiting to pass
the food trolley. A separate dining carriage
for pancakes and coffee. Blinds you can pull down
to mute the sun. A screen charting where you're going
and all the places you've come from.

I wish my mind was this German train; efficient,
orderly, running on time. And all these thoughts
traveling to who knows where –
chattering-eating-sleeping, quietly crying
or lingering at the window, lost in the face staring back.

Sally Traffic Reports on the Neurological Effects of Multiple Sclerosis

Today rising temperatures are causing delays
and a lack of concentration.
There are closures on routes between Mouth and Brain
creating a tailback of non sequiturs
and general misunderstanding,
whilst problems around Puttingonefootinfrontoftheother
are adding twenty minutes to most journeys.

On the stretch between Fingertip and Shoulder
numbness has affected driving and fastening small buttons.
Meanwhile, queues anticlockwise between Head and all regions
have resulted in problems remembering anything important.
From lunchtime onwards, there is a one-way system in place.

Fog in the Optic area has led to reduced visibility;
people are advised to avoid tiny writing, threading needles,
and foreign films with subtitles.
Noisy diversions on school runs
are generating widespread confusion
and faulty signals have caused a lack of balance.
During these severe conditions maintain space around you.

All routes between Head, Hands, and Feet
will be closed for the weekend following a day of overdoing it
and a late night watching box sets.
If you're heading out today, keep confidence and self-belief
fully inflated to minimise the risk of punctures
because fatigue has led to extensive congestion;
for much of the time you won't know
if you're coming or going.

Zoë Sîobhan Howarth-Lowe
Memory Shelves

Inside my brain I am constructing
memory shelves.
So many thoughts
jumbling
tumbling
rumbling
rolling around, a thousand thousand loose marbles
angry bees, humming for honey
and an elephant, sitting in my ear, slurping noisily.

I've Got Snakes Inside My Ears
and Bursting Blisters on My Brain

Man, I've got snakes inside my ears
and bursting blisters on my brain
I'm zoning in and zoning out
my thoughts all spinning everywhere
through a glass wall I try to hear you
but it's hard to understand
the people speaking to me
talking to me, total overload
I'm zoning in and zoning out
my thoughts all spinning everywhere
all conversation is frustration
and I'm struggling to connect
with people speaking to me
talking to me, total overload
with random thoughts
creative impulses exploding in my skull
all conversation is frustration
and I'm struggling to connect
the people play a social game
in which it's tricky to keep up
with random thoughts
creative impulses exploding in my skull
and hissing snakes with angry bites
injecting venom in my ears
the people play a social game
in which it's tricky to keep up
I can't repress these inner demons
'cos I hear them all the time
and hissing snakes with angry bites
injecting venom in my ears

eroding all my confidence
distracting me with rage and doubt
I can't repress these inner demons
'cos I hear them all the time
the stinging lectures of my aunt
that reeked of words that stank of truth
eroding all my confidence
distracting me with rage and doubt
the taunting bullies in the playground
shouty teachers in the class
the stinging lectures of my aunt
that reeked of words that stank of truth
the scattered fragments of the past
that are embedded in my mind
the taunting bullies in the playground
shouty teachers in the class
the friends I've hurt, the loves I've spurned
all pull me deep inside myself
the scattered fragments of the past
that are embedded in my mind
these vivid images so sharp
they prick my conscience, stir my thoughts
the friends I've hurt, the loves I've spurned
all pull me deep inside myself
I can't contain them, stretching, screaming
as they struggle to escape
these vivid images so sharp
they prick my conscience, stir my thoughts
the superheroes, evil villains
pretty damsels, wise old men
I can't contain them stretching
screaming as they struggle to escape
rampaging armies, squabbling politicians
suffering innocents
the superheroes, evil villains

pretty damsels, wise old men
I make up stories through my dreams
my fantasies are brought to life
rampaging armies, squabbling politicians
suffering innocents
burst out of me and take the shape and form
of words and with these words
I make up stories through my dreams
my fantasies are brought to life
in plays and poetry; pantoums, haikus
sestinas, sonnets, songs
burst out of me and take the shape and form
of words and with these words
I speak the truth; I am alive
I live for this, performing words
in plays and poetry, pantoums, haikus
sestinas, sonnets, songs
I am complete yet so alone
imagination rules my world
I speak the truth, I am alive
I live for this, performing words
because I'm itching to create
cut loose and let the demons out
I am complete yet so alone
imagination rules my world
through a glass wall, I try to hear you
but it's hard to understand
because I'm itching to create
cut loose and let the demons out
see, I've got snakes inside my ears
and bursting blisters on my brain.

John G. Hall

Burns on the inside

got home and found

my brain had been broken into
endgames were started on me

fire curtains brought down
false starts raining full stops

twisted right wing brackets
the days full of nights time

the sun turning into cold mind

me between the rock of ages
and the hardest word placed

grow up meaning grow down

freedoms our open prisoners
offered to me forced feedings

refusal taken as suicide noted

a kick in the teeth just a joke
they insist I get insist I liked

make me take their bad bets

got home and found that my
brain had been broken into so

here I sit my soul a damp squib
a blue touch paper untouched

my sky rocket still in the bottle
my powder burns on the inside.

COMMUNICATION

Communication is, by definition, a process involving more than one person. But when it breaks down, it is usually the person with the minority communication style who is judged to be at fault.

Different people communicate differently. Some people find it easier to speak than to write. Some prefer visual representations to printed words. Some people rely on gestures to communicate, others do not.

Some autistic people do not speak, but that does not mean they do not communicate. Naoki Higashida's 2007 book *The Reason I Jump*, and the 2020 film of the same name, offer insight into non-speaking autistic ways of communication and experiences of the world.

Rachel Carney is a dyspraxic poet, creative writing tutor and PhD student based in Cardiff. Her poems, reviews and articles have been published in magazines such as *Poetry Wales*, *Envoi*, *Under the Radar* and *Acumen*, and two of her poems have been shortlisted for the Bridport Prize.

Finola Scott was found to be dyslexic at a late age and both her children are neurodivergent. A recent winner in *Gutter Magazine*'s Morgan Competition, her pamphlet *Much Left Unsaid* is published by Red Squirrel Press.

Scarlett-Rose Summers is a performer, live artist, workshop facilitator and producer-in-training based in Manchester. Her work often explores her relationship with her dyslexia, dyscalculia, dyspraxia and Irlen syndrome, in attempts to embrace her neurodiversity as a gift.

J.A. Mickleburgh is a writer and teacher from Bristol who lives in Salford. Diagnosed with both autism and ADHD as a child, his writing touches on these themes and draws heavily on his neurodivergent special interests as metaphors for trying to navigate the modern world as a neurodivergent individual.

Jackie Carpenter writes funding bids, presentations and reports in her work for a homelessness agency, and letters to friends for fun. When she was in her fifties, a surgical but kind question uncovered the autism in her family. She identifies as neurodivergent and queer, and lives in Derbyshire.

Tracy Smith is an autistic writer who specialises in non-fiction based upon her focused interests of organisational culture, universal design, and neurodivergence in work.

Noeme Grace C. Tabor-Farjani has been published internationally and is author of *Letters from Libya: Memoirs-in-Letters* (2018), which chronicled her family's escape from the Second Libyan Civil War in 2014. She previously taught translation, children's literature and drama at Capitol

University and Humanities at St. Mary's School in Metro Cagayan de Oro in the southern Philippines.

Tricia Ashworth grew up in Burnley and gained a BA Hons in Creative Arts, drama major, at the University of Northumbria. She currently lives in Manchester and performs regularly in region.

Kate Fox is a poet, author and comedian whose work considers gender, class and neurodiversity. She is a National Autistic Society Cultural Ambassador, has performed on BBC One and BBC Two, regularly guests on BBC Radio 3's *The Verb*, and has presented BBC Radio 4's *Pick of the Week*. Kate has been Poet in Residence for the Yorkshire Festival, Great North Run, Glastonbury Festival and *Saturday Live* on BBC Radio 4. Her latest collection, *The Oscillations*, was published by Nine Arches Press in 2021.

Rachel Carney

The Blather

begins, as always,
        with a solid silver
line of thought,

        twisting, pulling out
        towards the light:

          fine as silk, strong, spooled
from the depths of the mind.

But then, as the mouth begins to open,
        it drops
          away,

leaving nothing –

        just a vast hole
of dread, and the hope that words

        (battered, crawling out
          on hands and knees)

might bring the silver back again.

A risk, then, yes, but every time,
still, I draw my breath
        and take that leap:

I hold on to the silver, try not
to let it slip,
        aware that,
if it falls away,

the blather is all I have –

         just words,

words

    words.

words gang up

drunken spider-writing hid a lot
but   the saying it
out loud
oh   the saying
a boyfriend would smile
pat my knee   then
correct me smiling
it's   linn oo lee um
tiddlyhum
I learned to say   lino

school was tricky
parallelogram / / paralellogram
with its pal corrr/oll/or/ry
redlorryyellowlorryred
I felt my tongue helter-skelter
those lls
for leather
pell mell

time taught me   snakey sneaky
avoidances   mouth-dances
those terradactyls & thesauruses
till I was saved
      well almost
by spellchecker
by tippytappy txt msgs

Wordsearch: Symptoms of Dyslexia

C	L	O	W	N	P	E	R	I	P	H	E	R	A	L	A	C	K	S	H
O	E	C	N	A	B	R	U	T	S	I	D	N	I	E	T	S	N	I	E
N	V	S	K	U	N	A	B	L	E	P	B	C	N	Q	O	G	E	F	A
F	I	I	N	G	N	I	K	W	A	H	A	Y	C	A	N	N	O	T	D
U	V	M	O	T	M	B	G	B	Y	U	I	S	A	B	Z	I	W	B	A
S	I	A	S	Y	E	U	Z	C	E	J	S	M	P	I	T	Y	R	O	C
E	D	G	I	F	V	N	S	D	N	D	U	U	A	L	L	P	O	Q	H
D	O	I	D	X	I	O	W	T	S	N	A	L	B	I	U	T	N	D	E
K	I	N	E	S	T	H	E	T	I	C	N	C	L	T	C	A	G	X	S
L	N	A	P	K	P	O	O	R	D	S	R	S	E	Y	I	L	M	L	H
N	S	T	I	I	E	G	I	F	T	E	D	H	A	C	F	O	O	Z	G
D	O	I	C	L	C	V	S	F	A	T	I	G	U	E	F	W	S	C	M
Y	M	V	N	L	R	I	B	T	R	O	U	B	L	E	I	L	U	I	S
Z	N	E	I	E	E	M	I	S	B	E	H	A	V	E	D	E	P	H	M
A	I	B	V	D	P	V	H	A	B	T	F	M	C	H	K	V	L	T	E
L	A	O	A	Z	E	C	G	T	N	H	X	A	W	A	R	E	B	A	L
G	D	K	D	Z	I	R	X	A	N	D	E	R	S	O	N	L	V	P	B
E	R	R	O	R	S	F	C	U	R	I	O	U	S	Q	C	O	C	M	O
C	Z	D	S	A	F	A	I	C	T	U	R	E	T	H	I	N	K	E	R
O	B	S	E	R	V	A	N	T	S	K	B	Z	O	S	S	A	C	I	P

CANNOT	PROBLEM	ERRORS
UNABLE	INCAPABLE	TROUBLE
CLOWN	LOW-LEVEL	DIFFICULT
SLOW	VACANT	CLUMSY
POOR	LACKS	LAZY
MISBEHAVED	CONFUSED	DISTURBANCE
	WRONG	

J.A. Mickleburgh
The Ancient Tongue

Day by day by day I read the arcane texts.
Immerse myself in cultures I do not understand
and never will
because all the people who understand my voice are gone
and some days, I don't even know if they were there.

I think to the memories that may or may not have been.
The uncertain laughter, the programmed replies,
the Turing test society demands we meet to tick a box
to fit in, to gain basic respect and
human dignity.

Aetatis suae viginti septem.
Anerrhiphtho kybos.

Such confusion. Such chaos.
A hive of misunderstanding and anger.
Resentment for the circumstances in which this occurred.
Maledictus vir matrem suam.

But all that can be done through this trek into the unknown
through the mistakes and the gaffes
is to enjoy the ride and hope for the
best.

If I had a magic potion

I'd want it to blot out all the words that people don't really mean
redacting them with low BLUUUHHHs

Gaps and gaps, and maybe some words would survive.
It would be fun

Some small talk might creep through because sometimes
I really do mean
'Nice to see you!' or 'Great look!'

The potion is made from:
a healthy dose of truth
a smidge of self-respect
a big top-up of purity

Take a small sturdy glass.
Start with your base of heavy truth
plopping doughy into the glass.
Sprinkle on a tang of self-respect.

Stir in the red fizz of purity
like blood orange San Pellegrino.
To mix, squash the truth against the glass.
Enjoy its silly-putty fart-noises

Drink down in one.
There is no smell. You only see,
can't taste, the effervescent orange
less flavour than water

How you feel when you drink it depends on who you are
The wholehearted feel invigorated, uplifted

A sly trickster will feel dark
churned up, as though they are just
starting with food poisoning
not quite sure what will come out of where.

Flow

Flow.
Hammering out a rhythmic beat
Tap tap tap
Flow.
Intense focus, laser detail
The writer orchestrates her vision
Flow.
Energised interest, full immersion
Spotlighted, laptop glow
Flow.
Words fill the screen, black on white
Craft absorption
Flow.

Noeme Grace C. Tabor-Farjani

Gethsemane

I am not the 2am girl awakened by night terrors
or some knock of memory visitors.
I am swimming deep with remembrances
in the waters of dreams.

I am not the 6am woman rolling her sleeves to slay dragons
or opening her eyes to smile at the sun.

By then I am all done. But I lay awake at 4am
choosing between going back to the waters and
to gather more strength or to romance sleep
or savour the seeping of dawn and endure
the birthing pain of morning.

Usually, I choose the contractions
the sporadic throbbing of flashbacks
followed by tugs of the present:
"Hey, the crickets are doing it in the key of F!"

Then the ache comes again of not knowing.
Struggle to squeeze them all out into the white
that glares empty on the screen.

Backspace, backspace.

Footsteps in my head, muffled voices.
"Those are from my '90s journal," I said to myself. "Passé!"

And then the 5am silence:
peep through the window
and wander, wonder when
shall my morning
come?

Contractions.
"Oh, when will things
get better, when it cannot
be the same again?"

Exhale through the mouth.
More contractions.

When labour is done I do not always find the birthing
of new words into the white sheet.
Sometimes or most of the time I just feel them in my heart.

So at 4am in the Gethsemane hour
I take some time and bits of pain
whether to rest or rise; either way
it makes me ready enough to face the day.

Tricia Ashworth

Dyslexic's Nightwear

In the seams of my negligées
I search for letters
try to entice them out
by whispering loudly

In the pockets of my nighties
I demand words jump out at me
predictably stubborn
plain lazy?

Under the collar of my pyjamas
I store phrases
never know when you will need them,
a good argument
or cheating at Scrabble.

In the cuffs of my dressing gowns
I hide verbs, nouns and adjectives
like peanut butter sandwiches
In case I get stuck on a fire place
Or hungry on a mountain.

On souls of my slippers
I write frustrating sentences
I flash them in the night
Enticing folk to look at me at
Sexy spelt Sxey.

What Could Be Called Communication

You might find them staying near the walls
or clutching their earphones,
rocking from foot to foot
and looking just above their audience.

They might be wincing at sirens,
saying "Pardon" a lot in crowds,
clutching the rails on angled walkways,
wondering at the calm faces of everybody else.

Sometimes they rest a foot on a crossed ankle
in such a way that others will click "Love"
in recognition when one of them
writes a Facebook post about it.

They might have coloured lenses
or squint perpetually into the sun.
They think everyone can see
the fluorescent lights humming.

Their eyes dart or fix
so they might be called evasive
or invasive.

They're stroking a finger,
twiddling with their hair,
tearing up paper, something
in a mesmerising rhythm.

They do not always recognise each other,
though are often to be found clustered
around tea urns,

outside where it's quiet,
in wombs

so they can perpetuate their tangents
and straight lines
build forests of themselves

where they communicate under the soil,
sending micellar releases of carbon and water
to those who need them,
passing on survival tips,
encouragement, warnings
in pulses of sound and light.

SENSES

Neurodivergent people often have atypical sensory sensitivities. We may be more or less sensitive than typical people to light, sounds, colours, textures, pain and tastes. We may have intense interests and find that certain sensory inputs disrupt that, or the sheer amount of sensory input may overwhelm us.

Some neurodivergent people are sensory-seeking, particularly enjoying certain textures, sounds or other sensations. Our sensory experience may be intense and satisfying, and being prevented from accessing it can be painful.

Some neurodivergent people have synaesthesia, their brains interpreting one type of sensory input through another. They may hear colours or taste sounds.

Anna Cotton is a synaesthete who has always lived a colourful life. When not tasting triangles and listening to lights, she is addicted to writing – it helps wring out her thoughts and make sense of the world. She has written three contemporary fiction novels and her story 'Dreadless' won The Campaign for Real Fear flash fiction competition.

C. Green is a writer based in the North of England whose work is inspired by the rich histories, landscapes and coastlines.

Emily J. Helen is a writer and poet, appointed as her county's Young Poet Laureate in 2017. She was featured as the 'chosen poet' for *Marble Poetry Magazine*'s broadsheet and her work is also in Turnsol Editions' anthology *Florilegium* and *Words & Whispers Literary Journal*. Her poem 'Somewhere in self-doubt' originally appeared online at selcouthstation.com.

Rachel Phillips was diagnosed as autistic at 47, having had a lifetime of feeling different and not knowing why. She works as a lecturer at Nottingham Trent University to fund her book addiction and feed her special interests.

Anna Cotton

Dreamcoat

Don't label me
disorderly
because I'm wrestling
with parasite coated arms

I'm chewing scouring pads
I'm inhaling prickly pears
don't tell me to cut it out
do you think I haven't tried?

I'm seeing cymbals again
the stars are C sharp minor
my collar's made of pins
each thread
hand-stitched by fire ants

This porcupine around my neck
is rendering me irate
quick
unpick it
from my straitjacket's nape

I've got my eye on Joseph's coat
it sings to me in spirals
but he won't play let's pretend
with the girl who swallows spiders

My condition is critical
so don't be alarmed
if my skin bleeds tangerine
and bruises technicolour

C. Green

Synaesthesia

Friday is Indigo
Velvet on the bare soles of your feet
And each day of the week its own colour

The word 'fern' makes your mouth water
Unfurling in lime sherbet fronds
Tingling under your earlobes

As you grow by each layer of pearl, you realise
This isn't how it is for everyone
How do others navigate this world

As you sketch an animal
You feel the lines trace onto your body
Slip into the sensation of its movement

As you write a landscape
That line of distant hills your shoulders
Fields of rippling wheat your moving skin

The word 'life' is clear
A chalk stream
Bright with water plants and minnows

The word 'death' is sparkling graphite
Holding a blue light in its centre

Gardens sing
Words are adventures

You follow the iridescence
Through your own pearling story

Emily J. Helen

Somewhere in self-doubt

there is a gaze unearthing / pruned petals in hands /
Zépherine soft / skin under a scab / my own defined holiness
/ a patch of grass dented with my hips / waiting for me to lie
down with it again / Cherimoya / power in eyes / power in
heart / power in mind / the oysters' gold and silver lips /
kissing me / stars, upright / a reminder / in harmony with /
the next stroke of night air

Rachel Phillips

Autistic Chameleon

She is the swirling colours of oil
on water, each view
a different tone, purples, blues,
grey to black and pink,
iridescent in the streetlights.

She moves like a hammock
strung between apple trees,
her swaying simultaneously
stimulates and soothes
in the soft, evening air.

She is the cloak that enfolds my body,
protecting me from the elements
as I walk along the sea wall,
breathing in such angry spray.

She is a murmuration of starlings, swooping,
turning, creating meaning
in shapes as night gathers them
to their roosting sites.

She is the power of water
to move from solid ice
through surging water
and, when heat is applied,
steam...

SOCIAL INTERACTION

Interacting with other people can be difficult, and can be exhausting. Keeping up with sarcasm, gestures, figures of speech and the coded ways in which other people often behave can be like navigating a never-ending maze.

Leading theorists of autism have declared that autistic people have no 'theory of mind' (Source: Simon Baron-Cohen et al.), that we cannot understand how other people think. But others have better understood the issue, pointing out that it works both ways: that typical people have as much difficulty understanding atypical people as the other way round. Autistic academic Damian Milton calls this the 'double empathy problem'.

Alex is a nonbinary autistic person living in the UK. The 'double empathy' of their poem's title refers to Milton's theory that as autistic and non-autistic groups both have difficulty understanding each other, this should be seen as a difficulty on both sides rather than an autistic deficit.

Freya Robinson is a 22-year-old writer and artist from Devon. Her work, which covers personal experiences of adolescence and autism, has been recently published in *Lithium*, *Take Care* and *Gems*, and is upcoming in *Unfiltered* and *Nerve*.

Pippa Hennessy is a writer and publisher who lives and works in Nottingham. She has published poems, graphic fiction, short fiction and creative non-fiction, and was selected as one of Soundswrite Press's three featured poets in 2019 with a collection inspired by quantum theory. She received her autism diagnosis at the age of 54, revels in her neurodivergence, and facilitates classes for autistic adults as part of Writing East Midlands' Beyond the Spectrum project. Her poem 'Superior Temporal Gyrus' refers to an area of the brain containing the auditory cortex – important for language comprehension, social cognition processes, and insight-based problem solving.

Tom Juniper is a genderqueer, autistic poet, sex educator and youth worker. They live in Sheffield, South Yorkshire, and have been published in anthologies by The Poetry Business, Three Drops Press and Pankhearst.

S. Reeson is 54-year-old multidisciplined artist who has suffered with anxiety since childhood. Identified as a historic trauma survivor in 2019, they are currently pursuing a more accurate diagnosis via the NHS.

Louise Wilding is a writer with ASD, ADHD and dyslexia. Regularly taking part in the Writing East Midlands' Beyond the Spectrum workshops, Louise loves being part of a community that just understands.

Skyler Saunders is a queer autistic poet, digital artist and freelance copy editor based in the San Francisco Bay Area, whose poems have appeared in numerous anthologies and magazines.

Artie Carden is a nonbinary, dyslexic, autistic and ADHD writer and editor who also makes regular video and blog content on disability, LGBTQ+ topics and books.

Alex

Double Empathy, Empathy

We speak two languages, you and I
Not in the words but the spaces between
A touch, a gesture, a tone of voice
The way your body moves unthinking
To signal things I can't read

And mine too, if you know how to see it
Both of us trying to learn a dance without hearing the music
At least I know I'm doing it.

Did anyone try to teach you how to make flappy hands
(to show happiness)?
Or how to look away
(to show you are focusing on my words)?
Or how to notice when I move my hands
(to calm myself from too loud, too bright, too much)?
All these skills you never knew you were missing.

When I meet someone whose body speaks my language
We notice, we click, we communicate
And in the moment that we understand each other
It feels more like dialect than deficit.

But we speak two languages, you and I
And yours is the only one they recognise
Therein are you trapped,
Boxed into a single perspective

I make adaptions for them every day
And they never call them "reasonable adjustments"
Never debate how much is reasonable
Unless they're being asked for it

But I'm tired of being too scared to speak
When I have things to contribute
Tired of trying, failing, trying, failing again
To translate my intentions into something you can
understand

* * *

Three body problem though,
Because life is not a binary
Sometimes it would be easier to give the benefit of the doubt
If someone hadn't stolen it already

And I'm tired of the hurt I'm causing
Tired of my faceblindness becoming
Someone else's microaggression
My misunderstanding becoming
Someone else's pain
Stuck in cycles, boxed into a single perspective
Until the past stops bleeding open wounds
Into the present
I don't know how to express this
I don't know how to fix this

But lately the world is barbed wire on old scars
Trauma-fuelled interpretations
Pouring fire on miscommunications
And I'm tired of us burning

* * *

It's a well-kept secret
That autism is prosocial,
It just needs the right context
Because we tend to value fairness over status
And the world cries for that.

We evolved within, as a part of the fabric
Just one of many ways to broaden the perspective
Nature is infinite, varied,
Contains multitudes, hates monocultures
Of course we get stuck
When we try to adapt to a world that
Doesn't have space for all of us.

What if we gave each other the benefit of the doubt
As we taught each other to build cycles of justice?

Freya Robinson

We Are All Running Up That Hill by Kate Bush

today I feel like a woodland creature going through puberty, wearing sunglasses and a hood in the supermarket so I don't have to experience other people.

do not tap on the glass, I look like a crime scene. if you do I will be legally allowed to pass away so speaketh not thine fucking crazy bitch, alright? shut up or I'm biting fingers off. just don't interrupt me when I'm staring into space, like, I'm busy. I am a weary ben affleck smoking in despair, I am playing classical piano in my haunted mansion at 2am, and potentially even running naked through the woods like a victorian woman with hysteria, you open wound. me and my brain are locked in mortal kombat, jousting at a bawdy tavern and wearing matching bracelets with the devil. I am right about to get frostbite from my own cold emotions, so please just leave me to be ugly in peace. a little raccoon asleep in a tree hollow.

I got rid of the whole day in the end. garbaged it up and watched it decompose. but for the first time I saw a shopping trolley in a river without empathising, and that was enough to make my heart swell, bursting the banks of the river with pride.

Pippa Hennessy

Superior Temporal Gyrus

tonight we're meeting at a party
you invited me
the month before last

the glow of inclusion
I'll get to see friends
I haven't seen Sue
since 2016

we're meeting at a party
you say it's easy to find

walk towards town
turn right by the pub
take the third left
fifth house on the right

your instructions melt
spread in all directions
I ask you to draw a map

sigh
OK, if I must

we're meeting at a party
I'd rather pull out my toenails
I remember now
why I haven't seen Sue

that time in the pub
she said chavs are scroungers
I called her on it
you poured vodkas down her
drowning ranted insults

I long to spend the evening
by the fire with a book

tonight we're at a party
voices stab at my ears
music rattles my bones

Sue's in the kitchen
talking to you

rhubarb rhubarb rhubarb
blah blah blah

your words drown
in a whirlpool of sound

tonight we went to a party
now we're walking home
turning left by the pub
my bones still shudder
my ears still bleed
you're talking to me

gabble gabble gabble
what did you say?
sigh

after drawn-out moments
I process your words

yes... thank you so much
a wonderful time

tonight I wish I hadn't gone to a party
would I have understood the crackling flames
and the quiet turn of pages?

Tom Juniper

Autisticus

This one is for all the
autists and aspies and neuroatypicals
people who find interaction so difficult
try to blend in but we can't with the crowd
we're either too quiet or SUDDENLY LOUD
at the wrong time.
But sometimes we want to fit in
what wouldn't we give to feel kinship with actual kin
but the din of the crowd that we tried to fade into
is too much, is too loud, it is too overwhelming
and all the well-meaning advice isn't helping.
We suddenly snap.
Oh and now it's gone silent
your noise is just background but our noise is violent.
When we get on your nerves it's because we're a let-down
when you get on ours we're just "having a meltdown".
We're supposed to learn strategies
learn how to cope
with your shit
when you won't even meet us halfway
well then how about nope.
Well then how about we're not a piece of a jigsaw
you're trying to solve and if you saw what we saw
you wouldn't be trying to take it away
with a fix or a cure or a vaccine to blame
because we can find beauty in numbers or trains
or the intricate patterns of pattering rain
or the way that the light hits the links in a chain
or historical plans of how Romans made drains
but you say we don't see the world
as it's meant to be.

Everything's wrong
and you say we've no empathy:
mate, we've so much that it's
causing us pain when we feel
all the tension around us flood into our brains.
Then there's nothing to do but lock in on the numbers
and patterns and theories and stories and trains
till it all ebbs away
and there's something like peace
but we can't be that way
at least not when you're there:
it's unnatural, unwanted, unhealthy, unfair
you have to police our responses
you don't seem to care about what's underneath
the blank stare
this world is so sharp that it cuts us.
But we come prepared.
There's places we know we can go when we're scared
and we know that it hurts you
to know you can't follow us there.
And I know that you think when I gaze into space
it's a source of disgrace
when you can't see the emotions
you think I should feel on my face
And I know when I look at you blankly I cause some alarm.
But it isn't my soul that you see in my face
it's my armour.

S. Reeson

Nothing Here is Working Any More

Here, unsocial, pretend *not*; instead
mind's the café, some small, busy shop where
previously
all those people stood, should *piss right off*...

between cloth mask and now
protective layer, sanitiser nuking every germ that's owned
it's suddenly a wrench

                                            to be alone.

Truth appears; once famous person hater
happily admitting failure:
resonance, togetherness

lies lost, between first need for
safety, common sense
second, inescapable as circumstance

                                            still on my own.

Don't make them Zoom,
can't control those terms... stuck in a square, digital
possession overwhelms egregious in tortures placed
everything in cyberspace

instead *please*, heart beats, random thrives
in which all this becomes, *survives*...

then everything
                        will be
                                  the same,
                                              as one.

Louise Wilding

Strange and Broken Forms

I hear you. I hear everything.
The rain drumming the window. The buzzing of the computers.
The air conditioning ruffling the paper on my desk.
Your voice swims in a sea of distraction that my ears as nets
    fail to catch.
I watch your eyes roll. Their derision scything the buds of my
    confidence. And shrink in the shame of knowing I've
    disappointed you.
Recoiling deeper into the shadows of myself, away from the
    electric glare of your annoyance.
I bend my reality to fit your expectations. I squeeze myself
    smaller and smaller to fit within the confines of my box.
    My place.
My body aches with the strain of it.
And yet, it's my exhausted mind that's expected to climb the
    hills of your incomprehension.
Why can't you bend your reality and pull me into the bright
    skies of understanding? Of your understanding?
Why do you expect these tired arms to do all the heavy lifting
    when they can barely traverse this conversation?
You demand attention.
I request awareness.
Less able to comprehend your words when forced to stare
    into the iron grip of your gaze. Witness to your
dissatisfaction. Prisoner of your condescension.
Hauling yourself above me, using the derision of others to build
    a pedestal as all-encompassing and as fragile as your ego.
Gilded in self-satisfaction. Raised by your own weakness you
    build monument to the thoughtlessness of your words
    scaled by those forced to carve themselves into strange
    forms.

Unnerved by my resistance.
Terrified of the minor inconvenience assisting me may require.
You wage wars with those too terrified to resist. And calling
    that victory.
I am listening; I do hear you.
Everything you're not saying.

This Isn't About My Childhood Trauma
(I Just Have a Crush on a Boy)

my emails have too many exclamation points.
you can probably relate. i apologise too much,
i use too many smiley faces in dms, i type in
lowercase enough that google docs doesn't
autocapitalise the word i anymore. i don't call
my dad enough, but my mom follows me
on social media so she knows everything
going on in my life. i'm looking for a new
doctor, a new therapist, a new person to ask
instead of google. it always seems like the
right thing to do, but then they ask, so what
brings you here today? and we only have an
hour, probably less since there's always the
small talk before that. an hour to unload my
whole life story. what kind of a first impression
does that make? where do i even start. i never
start with the big things. when i get to those,
i say them like they're an apology. i say them
like i know they'll have alarm bells go off in
their heads, and i'm trying my best to lower
the volume. i say them like, hey, please, this
isn't all of it. i'm more complicated than that.
i know it sounds like an easy answer, but if
it were that simple, i would never have come
here. i know how it sounds, but listen.
if you'd just let me explain—

I CNT SPK

I cnt spk 2 u rite now
I wsh I could
My wrds r strngled n my throat
I need u rite now
Ths is the only way I cn tel u
I hv 2 txt u

U shld sleep
U hv work
I gss u r mad.
Iv nvr dn ths b4
Nrmlly Im frced 2 rspnd
I knw u r not
No 1 knws whn im like ths
Its hrd 2 tel som1
Whn uv gne non-vrbl
Whn u dnt wnt 2 spk

Easier 2 giv
Shrt
Answrs

I wnt 2 tel u tho
I jst cnt spk
I cried lst nite
My thoughts wre loud
They wre
2
Loud

Ill prbably hv more nitemares
I will

I will wake u
If I need u
Im srry I cant say it

...
Gdnite x

Flapjack Press Publications

The Noble Savage	Tony Curry	£4.50
We Are Poets! [1]	Helên Thomas	£5.99
Tomorrow, I Will Go Dancing	Dominic Berry	£8.00
Planet Young	Gerry Potter	£10.00
The Wisdom of the Jumble Sale	Jackie Hagan	£6.50
Things I Did While I Was Dead	Rosie Garland	£7.50
Planet Middle Age	Gerry Potter	£7.50
Light Made Solid [2]	Ben Mellor	£7.50
Anthems and Album Tracks	Dermot Glennon	£6.50
The Men Pomes	Gerry Potter	£8.50
Wizard	Dominic Berry	£8.00
The Prequel to the Sequel	Working Verse Collective	£7.50
Fifty	Gerry Potter	£8.50
Tall Tales for Tall Men ...	Tony Curry	£7.50
Anthropoetry	Ben Mellor	£5.99
On Euclid Ave	J. Fergus Evans	£7.50
Strange World Odd Person	Rod Tame	£7.50
Livid Among the Ghostings	Anna Percy	£7.50
Spark, the Goblin Wizard [1]	Dommy B	£7.00
When Trolls Try to Eat Your Goldfish [1]	Dommy B	£7.00
The Chronicles of Folly Butler	Gerry Potter	£10.00
Beside the See-Side	Cathy Crabb	£7.50
The Dragon Who Hates Poetry [1]	Dommy B	£7.00
Selkie Singing at the Passing Place	Sarah Miller, Melanie Rees	£8.99
A Poet Called Dave	Dave Viney	£10.00
Poetic Off Licence	Hovis Presley	£10.00
Some People Have Too Many Legs	Jackie Hagan	£7.99
Li'l Book o' Manchester	Chloe Poems	£6.00
Pétroleuse	Steph Pike	£8.00
Lustful Feminist Killjoys	Anna Percy, Rebecca A. Smith	£8.00

Kaleidoscope	Laura Taylor	£8.00
The Story Chair	Gerry Potter	£9.00
Chuang Tse's Caterpillar	Dave Morgan	£5.00
Aaaaaaaaaaaaagh! Dinosaurs! [1]	Dommy B	£7.00
MUMB	Cathy Crabb	£8.00
As in Judy	Rosie Garland	£8.00
The Dance of a Thousand Losers	Geneviève L. Walsh	£8.00
Colourquest [1]	A.K. McAllister	£9.99
Travelling Second Class Through Hope	Henry Normal	£8.99
Accidental Splendour of the Splash	Gerry Potter	£10.99
Vaudavillain	Thick Richard	£9.99
Raining Upwards	Henry Normal	£8.99
Art By Johnny	Johnny Carroll-Pell	£12.00
Selected moments of machine life	Pete Ramskill	£8.99
Fault Lines	Laura Taylor	£8.00
Staring Directly at the Eclipse [3]	Henry Normal	£9.00
This Phantom Breath	Henry Normal	£10.00
The Department of Lost Wishes	Henry Normal	£10.00
Manchester Isn't the Greatest City ...	Gerry Potter	£12.00
I Can Draw My Alphabet [1]	Tony Walsh, Paul Neads	£7.50
I Meet Myself Returning	John Darwin	£7.50
extraño	Steve O'Connor	£8.00
Swallowing the Entire Ocean	Henry Normal	£10.00
The Anthology of Tomorrow	Various	£10.00
The Big J vs The Big C [3]	Janine Booth	£10.00
Strikingly Invisible	Henry Normal	£10.00
No Tigers	Dominic Berry	£9.00
The Escape Plan	Henry Normal	£16.95
The Beauty Within Shadow [3]	Henry Normal	£10.00
Jumping into a Waterfall	Anna Percy	£8.00
The People's Republic of Mancunia	Rik Jundi, Various	£12.00
Fighting Talk	Paul Cookson	£10.00

Read 'em and Weep	Thick Richard	£10.00
After the Storm	Rose Condo	£10.00
Can of Worms	Paul Cookson	£10.00
Best Adventure Ever! [1]	Dommy B	£8.00
Vitriol Works	Geneviève L. Walsh	£8.00
We Kid Ourselves	Tony Curry	£10.00
The Distance Between Clouds	Henry Normal	£10.00
How I Made My Millions	Rob Steventon	£9.00
Pig's Ear, Dog's Dinner	Paul Cookson	£10.00
Speaking in Tongues	Laura Taylor	£9.00
Job Lot of Rhymes	Cherry B	£10.00
Collected Poems, Volume One	Henry Normal	£16.95
Nail on the Head	Paul Cookson	£10.00
In Orbit, Back Soon	David Viney	£10.00
Songs of Submission	James Hartnell	£8.00
NeurodiVERSE	Various	£10.00
Collected Poems, Volume Two	Henry Normal	£16.95

[1] For children [2] CD also available [3] Audiobook also available

Available from flapjackpress.co.uk
and your favourite bookshops

Flapjack Press

Follow Flapjack Press on Twitter @FlapjackPress
or find us on Facebook and YouTube